Luna, Moon phases for little minds.

Written by Jessica Lake
Illustrated by Jasmine Bailey

ISBN: 978-0-473-59458-9
© 2022 Jessica Lake. All Rights Reserved

This book is dedicated to Sissy, like all women, she is a Goddess of the Moon.

To Mumma and Justin, who dance under the Moon as free spirits

and

to all humans and creatures who see just how special our Moon really is.

Have you ever wondered what those things are up in the sky?
Those great big balls of light that appear only during the day, or at night?

When you look up at night you will see the stars glistening above.
Like tiny shiny specs of dust scattered across the darkness.

The stars twinkle and fill us with wonder.

They help us dream, tell stories, and pass memories from one person to another.

During the day, the sun lights the way.
When you see its light rise, it is time to get up and play.

As the sun sets, Luna, the Moon climbs high in the sky.

Tonight, the Moon is full, and it looks like a great big pastry pie.

But not every Moon is full and rises at sunset.

The Moon has 8 phases.
Here are some ways to remember, so you never forget.

The New Moon is dark, with no light to see.

That is because it has its back turned to you and me.

Around midday the Waxing Crescent will rise,
with only a semi-circle of light seen by your eyes.

Waxing means the light is growing, so think of candle wax dripping off into a pile. The more that melts the more it is showing.

The First Quarter Moon will also rise from midday, being seen during the night and the afternoon day.

A week after the New Moon, half the Moon will light the sky or think of it as half a pastry pie.

The Waxing Gibbous you will see just before your night time rest, as it rises just before the sun sets.

As the wax keeps growing on the Moon, the word gibbous shows you there is more light than darkness to view.

The Full Moon is bright,
and all energy on Earth is high.

Rising as the sun sets, it lights up the night sky.
This is when lots of animals love to party and shine!

The Moon is full for just an instant.

But from Earth you will see it full for three whole nights.

Once the Moon is full the light will begin to disappear slowly.

As it moves through the phases to reach the New Moon again.

The Waning Gibbous waits for the sun to rise before it sets, so you may catch a glimpse in the morning after your rest.

Remember Gibbous means more light than dark, but waning means to dwindle or disappear. Think of it as the Moon going back to the start.

The Last Quarter Moon is also half full,
but the light is waning and dwindling still.

You may see this Moon with the morning sun,
as it will not set until midday comes.

At the last sign of light, the Waning Crescent will appear, as it means that the New Moon is near.

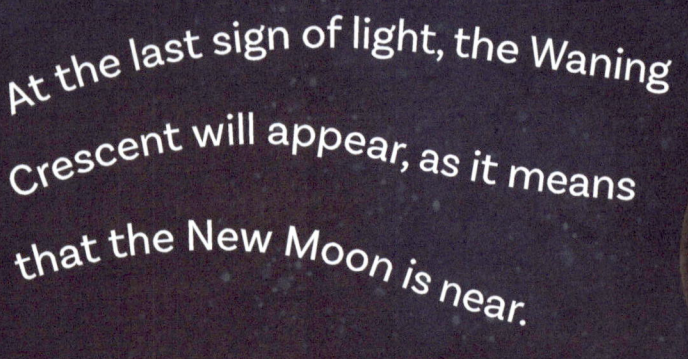

You will see a Waning Crescent on a clear day as well as at night, as it will not set until it sees the afternoon light.

Back to the New Moon to start the Moon's phases once more, not just once but another eight more. It repeats and repeats and will never change. If you ever lose track just remember this way.

If the Moon is showing in the afternoon, the Waxing phase is growing and the Full Moon is soon. If you see the Moon in the morning, you know the light is dwindling and the Waning phase is bringing the darkest night.

www.ingramcontent.com/pod-product-compliance
Lightning Source LLC
LaVergne TN
LVHW072118070426
835510LV00003B/121